POEMS DON'T DISCRIMINATE

REALITY CHECK

AVI

Made with ♥ on the Notion Press Platform
www.notionpress.com

To anyone who needs to listen...

Contents

Contents

Preface

I began writing out of despair, one melancholous day, in 2010, when everything seemed to not go well and I could not find an outlet for my feelings. These feelings were an amalgamation of loneliness and unstatisfaction that would not go away. Writing helped me get rid of them by expressing my views about several issues that relate to me, family, society, work, and life. Part of the reason that these feelings exist is because we humans create a false environment and then struggle to thrive in it. When nature has so much to offer then why do we run after man-made things, rules, and notions? which do nothing except harm us and the nature. Putting these thoughts down in the form of poetry and showing them to my friends on social media was the initial plan but this resulted in individual poems being astray in the digital space, and I was unable to bring the full effect of my words to the audience. So, I tied them together here in this book.

Acknowledgements

I would like to thank metal and rock genre music bands that inspired me to begin writing years ago. Their music and lyrics have been an inspiration for me to start holding the pen for poetry. I would also like to thank my wife who always loves and enjoys all of my poems regardless of the theme or style of each one of them. Finally, I would like to thank God or whatever energy is out there for bringing sadness to my life at the right times because without this I would have never started to write.

Prologue

Sun rises in the east
and sets in the west
yet there is uncertainity
about today
Leaves unfold infront of me
as flowers bloom
but there is no surity
on our longetivity
So stop your work
close your tech
and let the wind blow
past your hair
as the sun shines
on your face
Live the moment
as you enjoy these words today

Part I

1. The Native

I stand upon
a land: barren
miles and miles
of nothing
Earth has not been kind
but nor have they
Winds blow by
contorted trees
as I look
upon the demise
While they
'Revolutionalise'
'Materialise'
'Capitalise'
I cry tears
of the amazon
tonight

2. Our decline

Monotonous life
Netflix and chill
Just ain't right
Stuck in routine
staring at screens
day and night
Blurred sight
cramped hands
ain't no life
Working on screen time
entertainment on Prime
just no downtime!
Too much tech all the time
from daylight to twilight
The crawl of our decline

3. Burn

We don't need 5G
we need mind peace
We don't need more products
we need more forests
We don't need to go to mars
we need to fix what's here and ours
Humanity will not learn
until the last date
when it will be too late
For then
We will burn
mind and body to an urn
and yearn
for a single leaf of fern
Breathing heavily
to the point of no return

4. Busy

Stop glorifying this notion
else no one
will visit your grave
when the day comes
Buried or cremated
alone with your
human-made
accomplishments
Forgotten within minutes
your soul
shall wander
the halls of eternal despair
Unable to touch or connect
in any way
as your consciousness
frays

5. Technology

Was it years ago
life was good and slow
we were present in the moment
Less past, less future
feeling the nature
out on our bikes
a life of nurture
Outside...
playing cricket and football
followed by basketball
Inside...
boardgames and
just messin' around
But then came technology
tethering our idealogy
for now neither adult nor child
can even spell geology
without googling on their damn phones
and acting all smarty
Sitting around in family or friends circle
looking at their damn phones
staring into them like psychos

And wondering why
there is pain
in hands and knees
Maintaining social distancing
long before COVID-19 came into being
And wondering why
they're lonely and
can't sleep
It is a grim future
for you and me
as a user
For we are slaves to them
when they have no intelligence
imagine the mayhem
when they can think for themselves
And I know tech inside out
like hunger in famine
and thirst during a drought
By improving tech
you are no hero
trust me you do not know
the power of binary 1 and 0

6. Materialistic Life

People think..
buying a vehicle
a mobile, a TV
or literally anything is an achievement
Oh! how I laugh at their lapel
while staring unto the empty
dark stain on their souls
and upon the face of this world
People think..
having money in their banks
or saving a few bucks
to ruin their health
is an achievement
While the scythe in my hand
itches more than ever
waiting for them
at the other end
People think..
their made-up careers
matter
as-if they are fulfilling
some unknown and worthless prophecy

While I wait for them at a place
where none of this matters
they do not matter
and all that matters is:
how they treated others
for their limited time on Earth
The animals, the plants, the planet
and others less fortunate than them
wait beside me
as I wield my scythe
and my smile
is the last thing they will ever see

7. Dust and Bones

For finite years
you are here
in which
you slave away
Wasting time
for who? For what?
nobody
they call it money
While a single tear
flows down your face
and before it hits the ground
they would take it all
And you would be
alone and desolate
hanging by the bedsheet
breathing ventilator air
For who? For what?
nobody
Remember this
neither Nature
nor do robots care for this

8. Restrictions

Gone are the days
of calm and peace
Stuck in traffic
instead of relaxing
under a tree
glued to the confounded screens!
I miss the restrictions
of COVID-19
when the air was clean
and not a soul was to be seen

9. Not Covid

Time has come when eternity fails
when floods capture souls
wars rapture fabric of reality
heat consumes the bodies
plastic floats everywhere until north
of the Atlantic and Arctic
middle of oceans: Indian and Pacific
and south of Antarctic
Wherever eyes are laid upon
by you and me
there lies something
that shouldn't be
Money becomes a useless commodity
as we fall inside an abyss
made by none other than us
while the planet fills with the virus
that goes by the name: not covid-19
but humanity

10. Banknotes

Wash your feet
and clothes
in the flood waters
opening the gates of sorrow
Dangling on to false hope
see past the smog
feel the hot and cold
for your soul was sold
eons ago
Since the beginning of time
we have brought upon this world:
a slow demise
The decline of our only hope
So stuff your mouths
with banknotes
for they will be the last thing
left to swallow

11. Ambulance

They've got
"artificial intelligence"
but no common sense
"technology"
without touch or scent
"10 minutes delivery"
as people perish
in ambulances
"money"
but no time to eat
with their honey
"things"
with no happiness
"jobs"
with no satisfaction
"clocks"
and no time
They seem to be always in a rush
as the lines in their hands
fade away
inching them closer
to that ambulance

while their last thoughts
decay

12. Nature

Eternal rains come
as their droplets
devour the souls
that walk to this day
Looking behind
a scene from memory
fades away
unto nothingness
From the past
unto the present
standing upon a cusp
of rapid change
Riding towards
the stars of heaven
unable to turn back
having made this choice
centuries ago
From when we were happy
about the so-called
"Industrial revolution"
These words now
echo a different story

bringing upon tears
to our human race
in the face
of beautiful and deadly name
'Nature'

13. Communism - Capitalism

One makes you take fluoride pills
the other hides the same in water and paste
One forces you to follow their leader
the other manipulates you to follow their leader
One imprints their ideology onto your mind
the other uses marketing and advertising to do the same
One tracks your every move via spies
the other does the same through digital means
One ropes you in for life to work for them
"So you and family stay alive"
the other does the same
"So you and family have money"
One calls you 'comrade'
the other calls you 'colleague'
Do you see the hypocrisy?

14. Sugarcoat

People are more worried
about posts
than actual crime
A nude photo of a man
is considered offensive
but the same for a woman
means she's just expressing herself
Murderers, rapists, thieves and arsonists
walk freely
as complaints are registered against
posts and tweets!
'A fallacy'
They loot
and suck notes
out of tax money
with promises false
like sugarcoating everything
with adulterated honey

15. Earth

The water's up to the knee
there is no running away now
Decades lost
dispersing pollutants
in the atmosphere
and now we want to play it fair?!
The Earth beneath shakes
it trembles at our presence
like a host ridding itself of disease
Where will we hide?
when all in sight
evaporates in little time

16. Angels - Demons

Deaf from
the sound of rain,
winds swift past
contorted mind
Eternal sunshine
reflects on skin
darkness embraces
the cold within
A glimpse
into the eyes
of the universe
Entombed within
the two factions:
angels and demons
Circling above and below

Part II

17. Whiskey

Whiskey in hand
sensitivity in tooth
classical music
Acoustic note
wind chime
slight seismic activity
Roaming streets
feeling the sun
taste of food
Somewhere in the middle
lost in another realm
everything comes alive

18. Reflections

The green wood mirror
bugatti 1910 type 3
on a white wall otherwise empty
I stare at the reflection of me
gazing unto the darkness of irises
searching for light
beneath the abyss
Slowly I see you
caressing my silhouette
as we kiss
bringing light unto
this eclipse

19. Forgotten Rhyme

In the vicinity of my peripheral vision
I see a river flow
as the stars shine upon a dark sky
like pudding so black
Somewhere in the forest
I hear a rhyme
long forgotten
bringing a smile
Yet a hint of woe lingers
around my tethered face
For this rhyme
is not from my time
So how could I remember it
A rhyme
that I have never heard

20. Here not there

Why are we here?
not there
what are we doing here?
instead of somewhere else
Such a small fraction
of the never ending universe
from mars to jupiter
alpha centauri to neutron stars
All lie in the labyrinth of our minds
Like Black holes
our eyes are doorways
to our souls
and to universe's haze
unto which we stare

21. Universe

Seems every other day
every minute
every second
every moment
There is a spark
in the realms of darkness
Where light cannot leave blackness
stillness inspires
quasars shine
neurons fire
Ideas flow for miles
illuminated
tails of comets
hope surfaces
shooting star
upon the fabric of reality
intertwining universe
with human mind
Look for these similarities
only then you realise
that the universe is a being
just like you and I

22. 2 + 2 = 6

The moon shines
what sun reflects
somewhere in parallel universes
laws just ain't the same
Day is night
night is bright
it is a different sight
Dominant acoustics
muffled visions
two and two make six
Water is air
dark is fair
world with a different flair
So come join me there
in the middle of nowhere
amids the vastness
of universe's lair

23. Stones

Somewhere off
in a distant land
lie two stones
An emerald and a ruby
You chase them through time
Not knowing that they lie
within the realms of your mind

24. Unknown

Long long time ago
somewhere in the rubbles
of a ghost town
A man walked towards dirt
and started digging
in his suit
He was digging
not for diamonds, not for coal
nor for treasures lost or unknown
When came a light
from the future
burying the past
surrounded with dirt
A deafening sound
two hundred and forty one times
higher than the best soprano
of an Opera
As he found it buried
deep within the surface
of a town Unknown

25. Eye of the storm

Silence...
leaves blow gently
clear skies
weather warms quietly
Pressure lowers inside
higher outside
Winds...
hundreds of miles per hour
strike the bell tower
sounding dour
Hail...
they devour
the carcasses of those
who turn mood sour
Air or brain power?
As...
convergence sinks
winds to center
darkness engulfs
me semper
The...
coriolis force

deflects winds
from my presence
unto the eye-wall
within my vision
Leaving...
remanants
of calmness
within the eye
of my darkness
While...
scenes tumble
beyond the eye-wall's
blackness

26. Doppler effect

Heavyness in eyelids
eyes radiating
pressed lips
in the background play kids
on the road vehicle skids
A scene from memory
long lost
everywhere lies frost
bridges uncrossed
In the vicinity it moves
as sound waves surround you
red lights break through
a feeling of déjà vu
When the bat moves in front of you
upside-down he sees you

27. The Photograph

Smoke rises
in the air
surrounding you
in despair
Three klicks away
amidst
cloud and haze
Your picture
like a photograph
in dismay
As if Michelangelo
himself
painted your face
Transcending
through time
to this day
Hanging upon a frame
on captain's deck
to this day

28. Red

Shining flowers of orchard
reflect the beauty in you
I imagine through the eyes
of my consciousness: you
I imagine you
through the realms of my mind
through the paths tethered outside
through the world dark, cold and mad
I imagine a lone bench by the river
overlooking a park meadow
I imagine the scent of jasmine
as the flowers fall upon your hair
The look in your eyes
priceless
the smile on your face
like stars across galaxy's edge
So I move closer
when a kiss brings total eclipse
and day and night become the same
That moment
I still remember
for your lips were so red

29. Present moment

Leave the remanants
of past and
sorrows of tomorrow
For you never know
when you may see
your last rainbow
Live the present moment
as it unfolds
in front of your eyes
watch the sparrow fly by
Taste the sweet mango
sip a mochachino
dance the tango
have a burrito
Don't let future past
ruin the 'now'
For nothing else exists
and the world will disavow
you any minute now
So enjoy the present moments

Epilogue

When you're out there alone
nowhere to go
The beach, the waves
the beautiful sunrays
Play a sound to the seashell
rhyming it to your heart's content
For someone will listen to it
find you and like you as well

9 798890 261496

Printed by Libri Plureos GmbH in Hamburg,
Germany